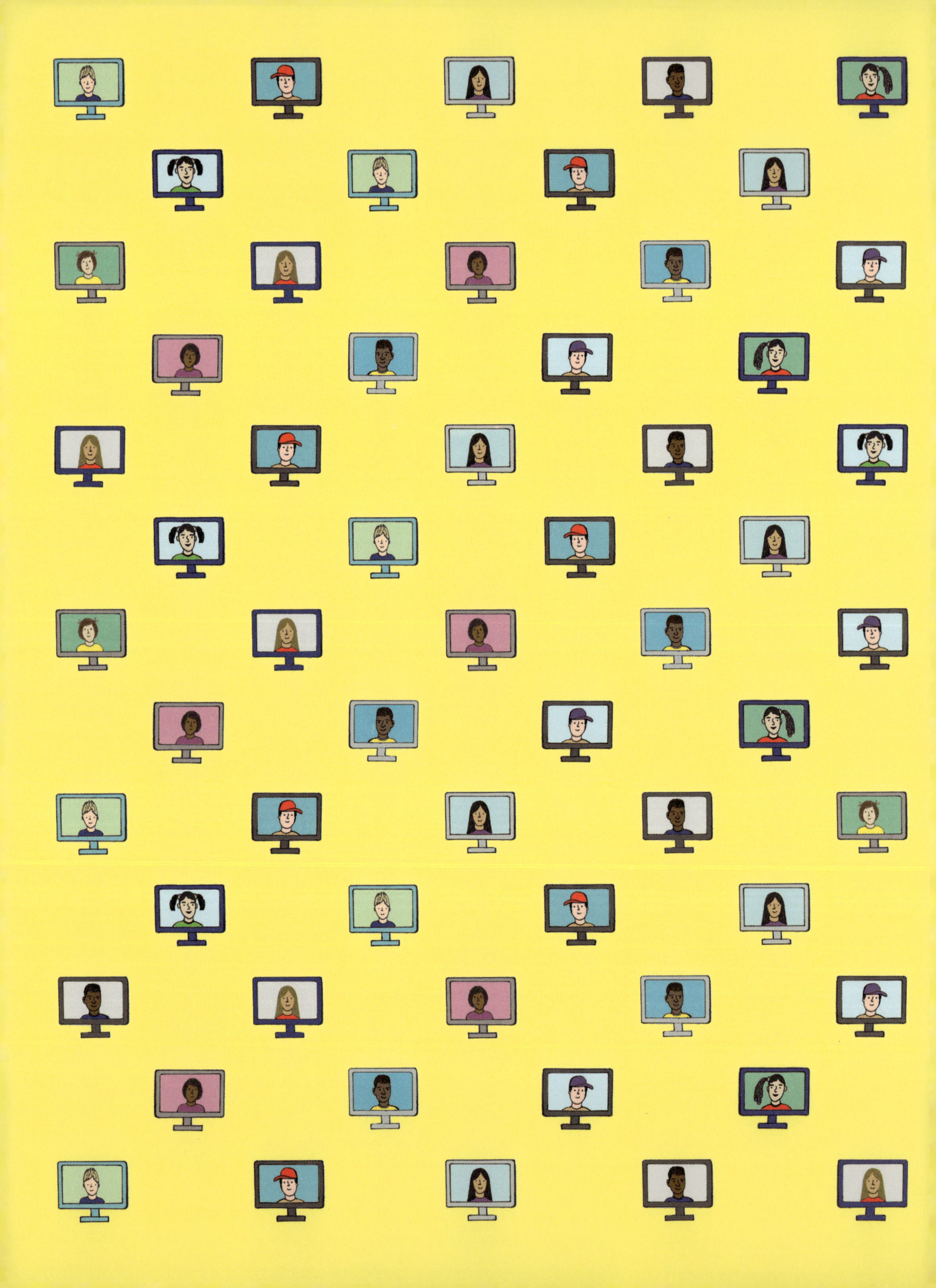

THE BRAINIAC'S BOOK OF

THE INTERNET

A NOTE FOR INTERNET BRAINIACS OF ALL AGES

The internet is huge, exciting and full of possibilities, but **BEFORE YOU SET OFF ON YOUR INTERNET JOURNEY**, be sure to take the necessary steps to keep yourself and your fellow internet brainiacs safe:

- Turn on your browser's parental controls
- Never share personal details or passwords online
- Speak to a trusted parent, carer or teacher if you need advice
- **T.H.I.N.K BEFORE YOU CLICK AND POST** (see page 50 to find out more)

HAVE FUN ON YOUR INTERNET JOURNEY!

Hi there Brainiacs! My name is Webby. I'm a total web-head, so follow me and we'll discover the amazing ways the internet keeps us webbed together. Let's get surfing!

THE **BRAINIAC'S BOOK** OF

THE INTERNET

WRITTEN BY
PROF. DR LARISSA SUZUKI

ILLUSTRATED BY
HARRIET RUSSELL

t&h

WHAT'S INSIDE?

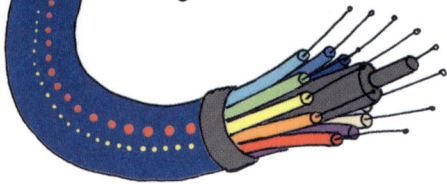

5

LET'S COMMUNICATE

COMMUNICATION IS A BIG PART OF LIFE - WE HAVE BEEN AT IT FOR THOUSANDS OF YEARS!

UGG?

UGG!!

IN THE PAST...

PICTURES
cave paintings

SPEECH
campfire stories

SYMBOLS
hieroglyphs

WORDS
hand-writing

Early humans needed to express their fears and share their experiences and ideas, just like we do today.

They found ways to make themselves understood with **SOUNDS** and then **LANGUAGE**. They used **PICTURES** and **SYMBOLS** and then **WRITTEN WORDS**.

GUESS WHAT?
THE WORLD'S OLDEST KNOWN CAVE PAINTING IS 50,000 YEARS OLD.

I CAN'T STOP TAKING PHOTOS OF MYSELF.

YOU HAVE NO SELFIE CONTROL!

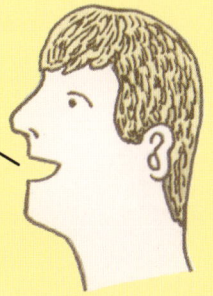

IN THE PRESENT...

PICTURES
sending snaps to family and friends

SPEECH
video calls and voice messages

SYMBOLS
emojis

WORDS
emails, texts and blogs

Fast forward a few thousand years to our hi-tech world. The internet allows us to communicate instantly with people on the other side of the planet.

The way we deliver our messages has moved on, but what we communicate is much the same.

In 2009, NASA sent thousands of text messages from the public to a distant Earth-like planet. It is so far away, any aliens out there will have to wait until 2029 to receive the messages!

GET THE MESSAGE?

DATA DUMP

FROM WAVING FLAGS TO WHISTLING WORDS, HUMANS HAVE FOUND SOME WEIRD AND WONDERFUL WAYS TO TALK TO EACH OTHER

BOOM-BA-BA-BOOM

TALKING DRUMS

In Africa, New Guinea and tropical America, people used drums to send messages to other tribes who were far away.

SMOKE SIGNALS

North American tribes sent messages in the form of puffs of smoke. Each tribe had their own code so that enemies could not understand the signals.

YODEL-AY-EE-HOO

YODELLING

This high-pitched singing was invented to communicate between mountain villages in Switzerland.

PHWEEEE PHWEEEE!

WHISTLING

Sylbo is the whistling language used on the Spanish island of La Gomera. It allows farmers to communicate across the steep valleys and hills.

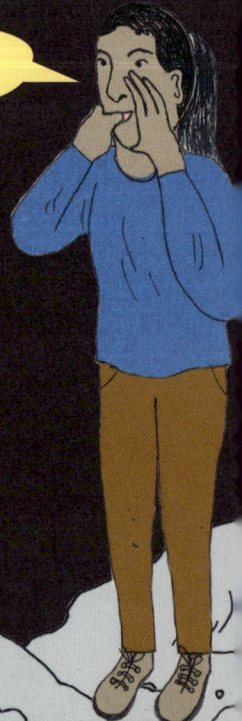

SKY WRITING

Adverts were 'written' with the vapour trails made by planes in the 1930s. The same technique was used during the 2020 COVID-19 pandemic to give health and safety advice in Australia.

Wash HANDS

BALLOON MAIL

Used by people in closed-off societies to float messages to the outside world.

FLAG SEMAPHORE

When two flags are held in specific positions, they represent letters. Created for the maritime world from the 19th century, flag semaphore is still used for emergencies today.

In the English royal court in the 18th century, ladies used their fans to 'speak' a secret language to the men. They could say 'go away' by dropping their fan, or 'I love you' by drawing their closed fan across their left cheek.

O **K**

THIS MEANS 'OK'

EAT YOUR WORDS!

In ancient China, secret messages were written on silk, wrapped in wax and swallowed. Then you waited for the call of nature!

SECRET SCALP TATTOOS

An ancient Greek king tattooed a message on a servant's head and waited for his hair to grow back before sending him off. When the messenger arrived he shaved his head to reveal the secret!

IT'LL GROW BACK

DOWN TO THE WIRE

WIRES AND CABLES WERE THE KEY TO LONG-DISTANCE COMMUNICATION

COOOEE!

SUCH FUN!

BRAINIAC HACK: SENDING SOUNDS

In 1672, Robert Hooke found that sound vibrations could travel through a wire or string from a mouthpiece on one end to a receiver on the other.

Invented in the 1830s, the **TELEGRAPH** machine sent electronic signals over a wire. Operators tapped out messages in Morse Code - short and long signals that represent the letters of the alphabet. At the other end, a machine printed the signals as dots and dashes to be decoded.

BEEP BEEP BEEEEEP BEEP BEEEEEP BEEEP

TAP TAP

In 1876, Alexander Graham Bell found a new way to transmit speech along a wire.

WATSON COME HERE...

COMING MR BELL!

Bell's **TELEPHONE** converted sound into an electrical signal. At the receiver's end, the signal was converted back into sound.

MAKE A CUP-AND-STRING PHONE

HELLO! CAN YOU HEAR ME?

What you'll need: • 2 paper cups • a sharp pencil or skewer
• string (kite string and fishing line work well, but any string will do)

• Cut a piece of string about 20 metres long.

• Poke a small hole in the bottom of each cup with the pencil or skewer.

• Thread the string through both cups and tie knots at each end to secure it.

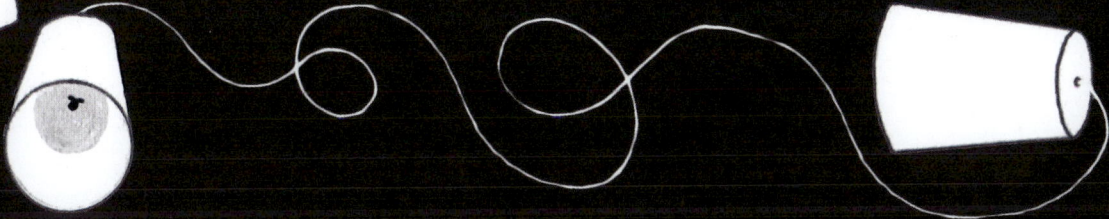

• With a friend, hold the cups at a distance that makes the string tight (making sure the string isn't touching anything else).

• One person talks into the cup while the other puts the cup to their ear and listens. Can you hear each other? What would happen if the line was cut?

EXPLANATION:

Speaking into the cup creates sound waves which are converted into vibrations at the bottom of the cup. The vibrations travel along the string and are converted back into sound waves at the other end so your friend can hear you. Sound travels better through solids, such as your cup and string, than through air.

MEET THE COMPUTER FAMILY

Every **NEW GENERATION** of computers that comes into the world is smaller and faster than before.

MEET YOUR PC'S BIG SLOW RELLIES...

FIRST GENERATION

Eniac, the first electronic computer, filled a big room. It did **5,000 CALCULATIONS** per second.

VACUUM TUBE   **BOOM!**

Early computers used thousands of fragile glass **VACUUM TUBES**. These gobbled electricity, got very hot and often exploded!

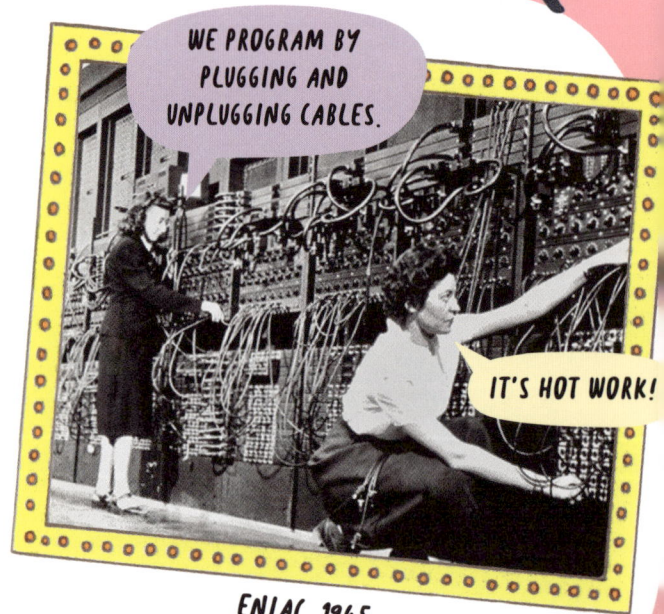

> WE PROGRAM BY PLUGGING AND UNPLUGGING CABLES.

> IT'S HOT WORK!

ENIAC, 1945

SECOND GENERATION

Unreliable vacuum tubes were replaced with **TRANSISTORS**. Now computers were able to process and store more information.

Only governments and big businesses could afford to buy computers.

TRANSISTOR

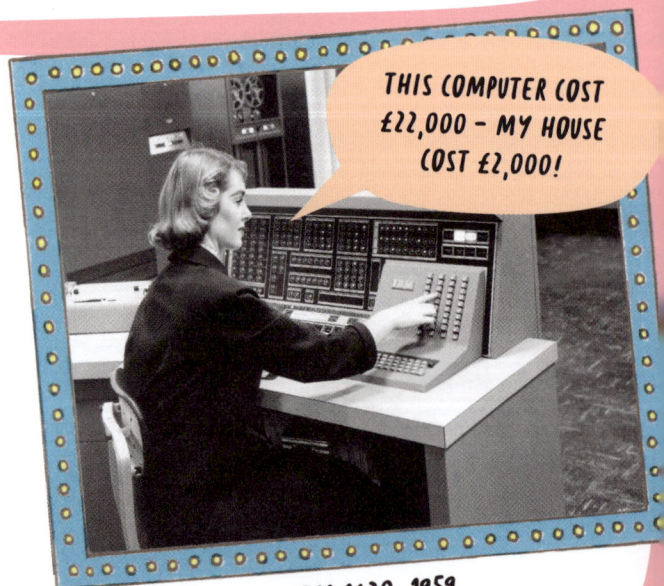

> THIS COMPUTER COST £22,000 – MY HOUSE COST £2,000!

IBM 1620, 1959

(IN 1959 £22,000 WAS LIKE £650,000 IN TODAY'S MONEY)

THIRD GENERATION

Transistors became smaller and faster, and so did computers. Lots of transistors could be contained on one small **CHIP**.

INTEGRATED CIRCUIT, OR CHIP

OFFICE COMPUTER, 1960S – 70S

FOURTH GENERATION

Personal computers, or **PCS**, were first used at home. These computers used **MICRO CHIPS**. One chip contained 5,000 transistors.

MICRO CHIP

APPLE MACINTOSH, 1984

happy birthday!

FIFTH GENERATION

Modern computers are portable and speedy, with millions of transistors. They can do **BILLIONS OF TASKS** every second!

SMARTPHONE

TABLET

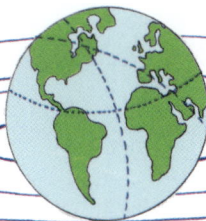

DELL LAPTOP, 2020

THEN AND NOW

ENIAC USED AS MUCH ELECTRICITY AS 3,000 MODERN LAPTOPS!

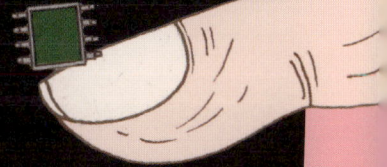

A COMPUTER THAT FILLED A WHOLE ROOM IN THE 1940S CAN NOW FIT ON A TINY CHIP!

80 years ago computers did not even exist. Today there are over 2 billion computers in the world! That's making my head spin!

MAKING THE WORLD'S BIGGEST NET

NOT FOR FISH OR FOOTBALLS – JUST BILLIONS OF COMPUTERS. IT'S THE INTER-NET!

NEED-TO-KNOW FACTS

A **NETWORK** connects two or more computers electronically so that they can communicate.

The **INTERNET** is an enormous network that connects computers all over the world.

HOW DID IT BEGIN?
In the **1950S** and **1960S**, companies in the USA needed to share information between employees. They created **NETWORKS** to connect their computers.

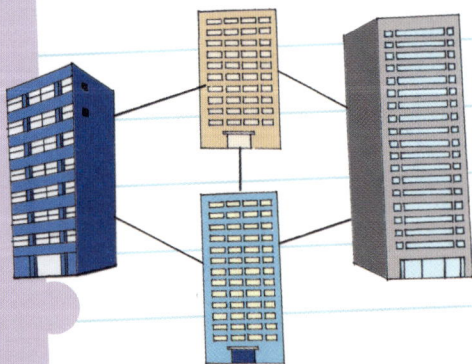

In the **1970S**, networks grew to allow **BIG ORGANISATIONS** to send messages between computers in different branches and offices.

In the **1980S**, **PCS** became popular and the internet spread across the world.

TODAY the internet connects **FIVE BILLION** users worldwide.

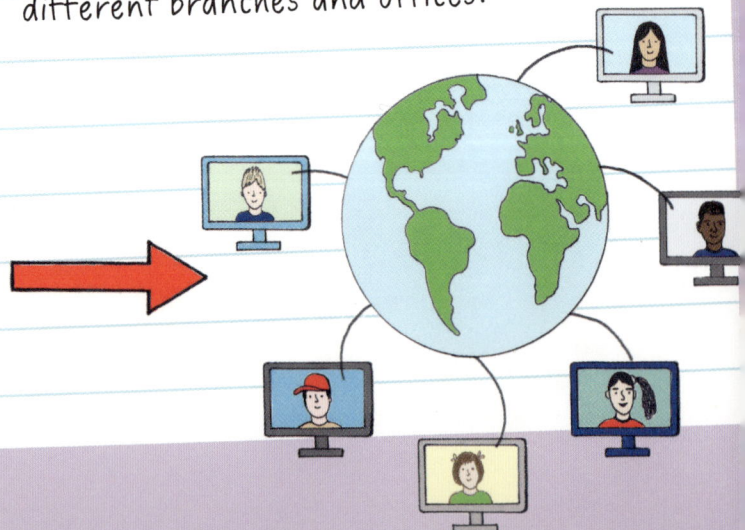

HOW DO TREES GET ON THE INTERNET?

THEY LOG ON!

MEET THE PARENTS...

... and get to know their rules!

THE 'MOTHER OF THE INTERNET'

In 1984, network engineer **RADIA PERLMAN** helped to grow the internet. She wrote rules to let information travel across a computer network using the best route. She called her invention **SPANNING TREE**. She even wrote a poem to go with it!

I THINK THAT I SHALL NEVER SEE A GRAPH MORE LOVELY THAN A TREE. A TREE WHOSE CRUCIAL PROPERTY IS LOOP-FREE CONNECTIVITY...

THE 'FATHERS OF THE INTERNET'

In 1974, top computer scientists **VINT CERF** and **BOB KAHN** had to find a way for different machines to understand one another and share information.

They set up a common set of rules, called **PROTOCOLS**, that built the internet that we know today.

SHARE NICELY

It took Radia Perlman just two days to create her Spanning Tree Protocol. That's tree-mendous!

15

INVENTING THE WORLD WIDE WEB

MEET THE TECHY SUPERHERO WHO CHANGED THE WORLD

British computer scientist **TIM BERNERS-LEE** invented the **WORLD WIDE WEB** in 1991 to solve a problem...

THE PROBLEM

Tim worked with scientists from around the world who wanted to **SHARE IDEAS**. Unfortunately, they all used different computer systems, so their machines could not communicate.

I DON'T UNDERSTAND

ONE LANGUAGE

Tim invented **HTML** - a language that all computer systems can understand. This meant that scientists could share information by connecting to the **INTERNET** and putting it 'online'.

FIND AND FETCH

Tim came up with the **URL** - a unique **ADDRESS** for every item put on the internet. He also invented **HTTP** - a way for **FETCHING** the items from their online location.

>> FLIP FORWARD TO PAGE 26 TO FIND OUT MORE ABOUT COMPUTER LANGUAGES

The **WORLD WIDE WEB** was such a success, Tim's invention was given away for everyone to use for **FREE**! Within a few years, one website had turned into millions. Now anything you need to know is just a click away!

Wow! The web is definitely the best place to learn about spiders.

TRY THIS

INTERNET TREASURE HUNT

Search the internet to discover some of the things you can learn for free:

1. 'What did Hubble see on my birthday?'
Find the NASA web page where you can view photos taken by the Hubble Telescope every day of the year!

2. 'How do I make text bold in HTML?'
Discover the tag used to change plain text into bold text. Girls Who Code offer free coding activities if you want to learn more.

3. 'How do I draw a football panda?'
You can learn to draw just about anything in free online drawing tutorials created by illustrators.

GUESS WHAT?
YOU CAN CHECK OUT THE VERY FIRST WEBSITE THAT TIM PUT ON THE WEB. SEARCH FOR 'INFO.CERN.CH' TO SEE HOW IT LOOKED.

IT'S NOT THE NET

DON'T GET THE WEB IN A TANGLE WITH THE NET. DISCOVER THE DIFFERENCE...

NEED-TO-KNOW FACTS

It's possible to use the **INTERNET** without being on the **WEB**, however it's not possible to browse the web unless you are '**ONLINE**' and connected to the internet.

The **WORLD WIDE WEB** (or web) is just one of the **SERVICES** available on the **INTERNET** - but it is definitely the most popular!

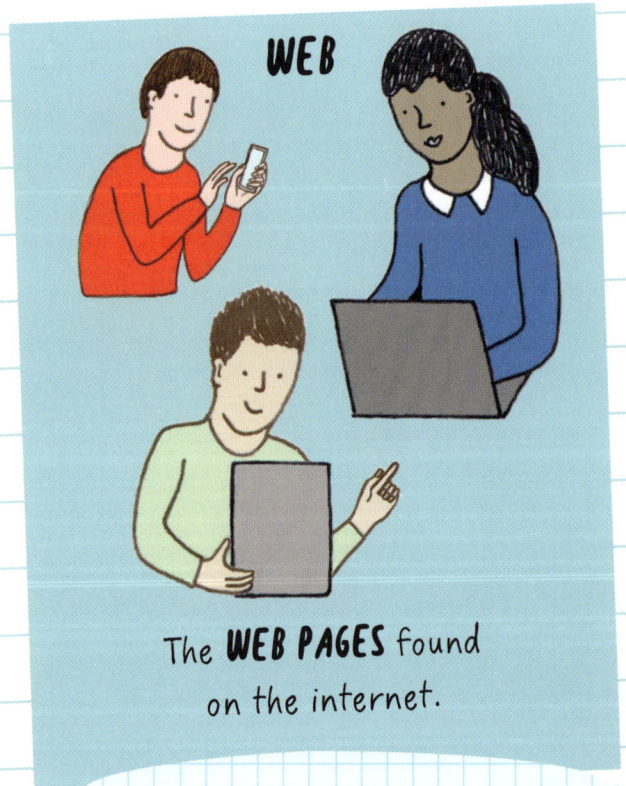

INTERNET

The huge **NETWORK** that connects computers all over the world.

WEB

The **WEB PAGES** found on the internet.

Got it! The web is inside the net! A version of the internet was in use before the web was invented in 1991, but its creation turned us all into internet users!

WHAT'S BIG, HAIRY AND ALWAYS ONLINE?

AN INTERNYETI!

TIME ONLINE

Fast forward to today and using **THE INTERNET** involves much more than sharing information between friends.

WATCH A MOVIE ON TV WITH A SET-TOP BOX

SEND AN EMAIL

PLAY A GAME ON A MOBILE PHONE

SHOP ONLINE

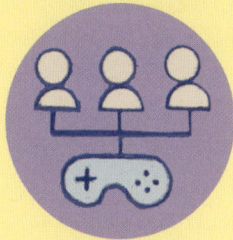

PLAY A MULTI-PLAYER GAME

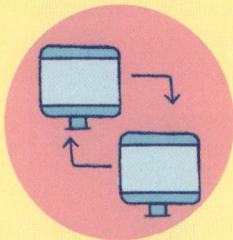

CONNECT TO ANOTHER COMPUTER

READ A BLOG

WATCH VIDEOS

INSTANT MESSAGE A FRIEND

RESEARCH A SCHOOL PROJECT

SEND A WEBMAIL

ONLINE SEARCH AND FIND

YOU CAN EXPLORE THE WEB WITHOUT TAKING A SINGLE STEP!

Computer programs do the hard work for you.

BROWSING

A **WEB BROWSER** is a program that uses the internet to connect to the web. It displays the words, pictures and videos on a website. There are lots of different web browsers.

I'M BROWSING FOR BROWSERS

GOOGLE CHROME

FIREFOX

MICROSOFT EDGE

OPERA

SAFARI

I'M GOING TO GIVE THIS ONE A GO

YAHOO

DUCK DUCK GO

BING

ASK

GOOGLE SEARCH

SEARCHING

There are nearly two billion websites on the web. A **SEARCH ENGINE** program helps you find what you are looking for quickly. Millions of results come up in less than a second!

There are lots of different search engines to choose from. Some browsers have a search bar too.

BEFORE YOU SEARCH ONLINE, ASK AN ADULT TO SET UP PARENTAL CONTROLS AND FILTERS FOR YOUR PROTECTION.

TRY SEARCHING FOR THE SAME THING USING DIFFERENT **SEARCH ENGINES**. ARE THE RESULTS THE SAME OR DIFFERENT?

CREEPY 'CRAWLERS'

A search engine uses programmed 'CRAWLERS' that scan the web for new and updated websites and add them to the search engine's huge INDEX. When you make a search, the crawlers explore the index, looking for web pages that best match what you're looking for. It's like going on an internet scavenger hunt! Have a go at being a super-searching 'crawler' with this game!

YOU'LL NEED: a notepad, a pen, 6 items you take to school each day, a stopwatch, a friend

1. Make a list of your school items.

2. Ask a friend to hide the 6 items around the house.

3. Get your friend to start the stopwatch timer, and go searching! Start in the room closest to you.

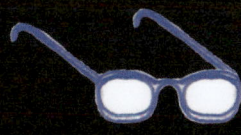

4. When you find an item, tick it off your list and make a note of which room you found it in.

Around the world, 99,000 search requests are typed into Google's search engine every single second!

5. Report back! Bring your search results list back to your friend. How fast was your search? Now search again. Now you know where to look, you'll be much faster!

TOP TIP

SOMETIMES WEBSITES MOVE AROUND THE INTERNET. LIKE MOVING HOUSE, THEY MIGHT CHANGE ADDRESS, SO THE CRAWLER NEEDS TO SEARCH AGAIN TO FIND THEIR NEW HOME.

LET'S GO SURFING

YOU DON'T NEED TO GET WET TO SURF ACROSS OCEANS OF WEB PAGES

CATCHING WEB WAVES

You travel around the web by clicking on **HYPERLINKS**, or links.

On a computer, when you hover over a hyperlink your **MOUSE CURSOR** (arrow) turns into a pointing hand. On your phone or tablet you use your actual finger to tap on and open a link.

A hyperlink on a web page might be:

WORD

an underlined word...

CLICK

a button...

a photo or a picture...

A hyperlink can take you to from one web page to the next...

... or it can whiz you to another website.

SURFING

CLICK

WHERE TO SURF

CLICK

HOW TO SURF

CLICK

CLICK

FIND A SURF BOARD

ONLY CLICK ON LINKS FROM SOURCES THAT YOU TRUST.

FAR FROM HOME

With so much to look at on the web, it's easy to click away and end up a long way from where you started!

Click the **BACK BUTTON** at the top left of the browser window until you get back to where you began.

MAGIC LINKS

Hyperlinks are found in all sorts of computer files, not just websites. Clicking on them opens the internet and transports you to the linked web page in the blink of an eye.

How did that happen? One minute I was looking at music fansites, I took a detour through hand dryers and I've ended up on a site about ancient toilets!

ADD A LINK

Hyperlinks can be added to emails and text documents. Clicking on them opens the internet and transports you to the linked web page. Use your search engine to get instructions on how to add a link. For example, type **'HOW DO I INSERT A HYPERLINK IN MICROSOFT WORD?'** into the search bar.

WORD DOCUMENT

My favourite hobby:
I go surfing with my mum at the surf school at our local beach.

EMAIL

To: Grandma
From: Elsie@icloud.mail
Subject: Birthday present

Dear Grandma
Thanks so much for my birthday money.
I spent it on a new surfboard.
I can't wait to try it!

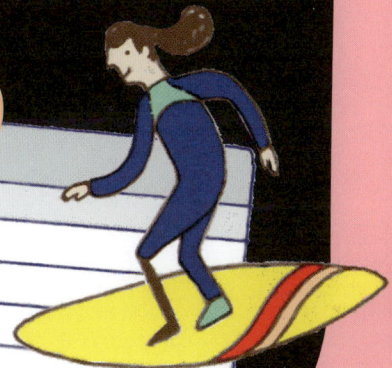

DATA DUMP

INTERNET TIME MACHINE
TURN BACK TIME TO SEE HOW FAR THE INTERNET HAS COME

1969 – MYSTERY MESSAGE

The first ever internet message is sent from a computer in Los Angeles, USA, to another computer hundreds of miles away. What does it say? Well, it's meant to be 'LOGIN' but the system crashes after the first few letters, so it just says... 'LO'

:–* O:-)

I-) :-! :'-(

1982 – ARE YOU JOKING?

Computer scientist Scott Fahlman notices that people are taking online messages the wrong way. He suggests using :-) and :-(to distinguish between jokes and serious posts. Today we type **EMOTICONS** for all kinds of emotions. Do you know what these emoticons mean?

1993 – STREAMING HOT COFFEE

Scientists at Cambridge University, England, set up the first **WEB CAM** to monitor a coffee pot! People are tired of turning up to find the pot empty, so they find a techy solution to their coffee cravings. Modern webcams are more interesting. Why not watch Woolong Valley Nature Reserve's adorable pandas at

https://explore.org/livecams/panda-bears/china-panda-cam-1

1994 – BANKING ON BOOKS

Jeff Bezos quits his job in banking to open the first ever **ONLINE BOOKSTORE** from his garage in Seattle, USA. Today Amazon is Earth's biggest online shop!

2001 – SIT AND SURF

Bury St Edmunds in Suffolk, England becomes the first town in the world where people can connect to the internet outdoors. A regular **PARK BENCH** is converted into a cyber seat, allowing visitors to log on with their laptops.

2005 – ME AT THE ZOO

On April 23, the first ever video is uploaded to **YOUTUBE** by its co-founder Jawed Karim. He stands by the elephants at San Diego Zoo in California and talks about their trunks!

SEARCH FOR: 'Me At The Zoo YouTube'

Today, the internet is everywhere! You can check emails on the climb up Mount Everest or post a penguin pic from the South Pole. Even astronauts on the International Space Station have the net, and will on the Moon soon, too.

01100010 01100101 01100101
01110000 00100000 01100010
01101111 01101111 01110000

HOW TO SPEAK 'COMPUTER'

COMPUTERS DON'T SPEAK OUR LINGO, BUT WE CAN COMMUNICATE WITH THEM IN CODE!

WHAT?!

BRAINIAC HACK: COMPUTER CODES

Computers understand one language – **BINARY CODE**. It's made up entirely of 1s and 0s!

Programmers use code to create websites. They don't write 0s and 1s, they use **PROGRAMMING CODES**, which are more like normal language.

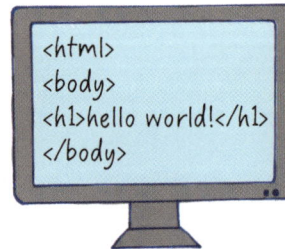

A program called a **COMPILER** translates everything into binary code.

NOW I UNDERSTAND!

```
<html>
<body>
<h1>hello world!</h1>
</body>
```

PROGRAMMING CODE

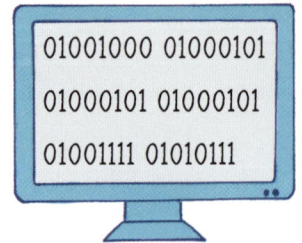

```
01001000 01000101
01000101 01000101
01001111 01010111
```

BINARY CODE

COMPILER TRANSLATES

BUILDING WEBSITES

HTML code is used for most websites. It tells the browser how to display the words and pictures. Other codes can be used to add colourful designs or animations.

I'M USING PYTHON CODE TO MAKE A WEBSITE ABOUT MY PET SNAKE!

HTML

JAVA SCRIPT

JS

RUBY

PHP

php

CSS

PYTHON

<< FLIP BACK TO PAGE 16 TO SEE WHO INVENTED HTML

CRACK THE CODE!

In binary code, strings of 1s and 0s represent numbers and letters.
Use the code converter to unravel the riddle.

BINARY CODE CONVERTER

A	01000001	N	01001110
B	01000010	O	01001111
C	01000011	P	01010000
D	01000100	Q	01010001
E	01000101	R	01010010
F	01000110	S	01010011
G	01000111	T	01010100
H	01001000	U	01010101
I	01001001	V	01010110
J	01001010	W	01010111
K	01001011	X	01011000
L	01001100	Y	01011001
M	01001101	Z	01011010

This has no doors but it has keys.
This has no rooms but it does have a space.
You can enter but you can never leave.
What is it?

01000001   01001011 01000101
01011001 01000010 01001111
01000001 01010010 01000100

REVEAL THE CODE

You can uncover the HTML code behind any website.

1. Open a website and click on a blank area.

2. On a PC: Hold down **CTRL** and press **U**.

On a Mac: hold down **COMMAND** and **OPTION** and press **U** (or **COMMAND** and **U** in some browsers).

3. A new tab will open up, displaying the HTML.

FOUND IT!

CAN YOU FIND ME?

EASY! EVERYONE AND EVERYONE ON THE INTERNET HAS AN ADDRESS

YOU'VE GOT MAIL!

Sending an **EMAIL** is like posting a letter electronically. A postal address and an **EMAIL ADDRESS** both contain all the details needed to deliver your mail.

Unlike post, email is **INSTANT** AND you can open your mail when you're not at home!

J. Smith
Reader Avenue
Booksville
AB1 2CD

joesmith123@coolmail.com

YES! I'VE BEEN PICKED FOR THE MATCH!

PING!

An **EMAIL ADDRESS** has two parts:

joesmith123 @ coolmail .com

The **USERNAME** is usually your name. People often add initials or numbers to make it unique.

The **DOMAIN NAME** is the company, school or organisation that you get your email through.

@

In 1971, when email was just starting, a tech engineer needed a way to separate the username from the domain name. It had to be a symbol that was quick and memorable - they chose @!

28

KNOWN BY NUMBERS

Every device connected to the internet has a unique number called an internet protocol address, or **IP ADDRESS**.

IP ADDRESSES are four numbers separated by dots, like this:

192.158.1.38

THE POSTCODE ON MAIL IDENTIFIES A BUILDING OR STREET

AN IP ADDRESS IDENTIFIES A SMARTPHONE, TABLET OR COMPUTER

J. Smith
Reader Avenue
Booksville
AB1 2CD

192.158.1.38

PING!

Every website on the internet has a **WEB ADDRESS**. It also has an **IP ADDRESS**.

https://www.websitename.co.uk ➡️ 82.129.90.111

THE CODE USED TO COMMUNICATE BY THE INTERNET

WORLD WIDE WEB

DOMAIN NAME

COUNTRY CODE

COMPUTERS USE THE IP ADDRESS TO LOCATE THE WEBSITE

Some people have got rich by buying and selling **DOMAIN NAMES** - sometimes by accident. The Tesla car company paid someone **$11 MILLION** for 'tesla.com'. It belonged to a fan of the inventor Nikola Tesla. He had bought it before Tesla cars even existed!

GUESS WHAT? DOMAIN NAMES WERE INVENTED BECAUSE HUMANS FIND BIG NUMBERS HARD TO REMEMBER!

DATA DELIVERY

A SPEEDY SERVICE IS WHIZZING WORDS AND PICTURES ACROSS THE WORLD

1. WHAT IS DATA?

DATA is words, images, videos, sounds - anything that is stored and displayed on a tablet, smartphone or computer.

I'M GOING TO SEND THIS GRUMPY CAT TO MY FRIEND.

2. DATA PACKETS

Before data can be sent it is converted into **BINARY CODE** (1s and 0s) and broken into small pieces, called **PACKETS**.

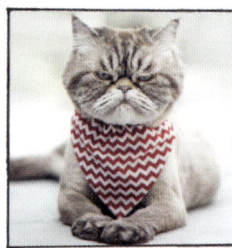

01101101 01
100101 0110
1111 011101
11 00001010

YOUR DATA

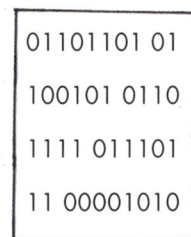

COMPUTER DATA

4. SEND THE DATA

Follow an email to see the route data takes across the internet.

Jess@coolmail.co.uk

Hi Sam,
Who does this cat
remind you of? LOL

ROUTERS check the IP address and choose the best path through the internet.

PACKETS enter the internet and 'hop' from router to router, taking different paths.

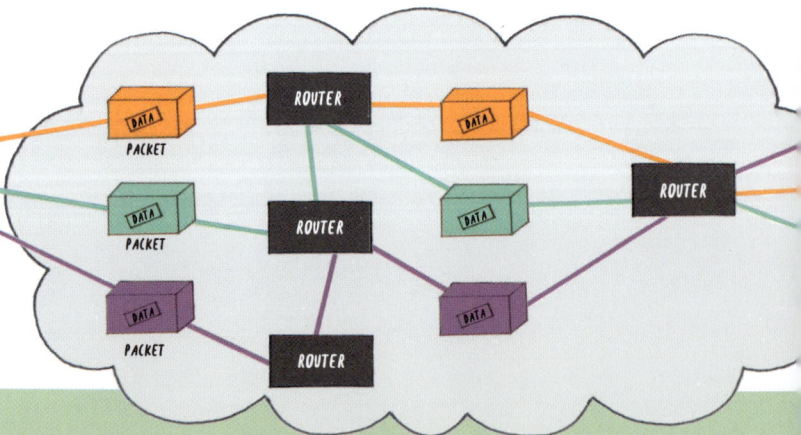

ROUTER

DATA PACKET · ROUTER · DATA · ROUTER · DATA PACKET · ROUTER · DATA · ROUTER · DATA PACKET · ROUTER · DATA

<< FLIP BACK TO PAGE 26 TO FIND OUT ABOUT BINARY CODE

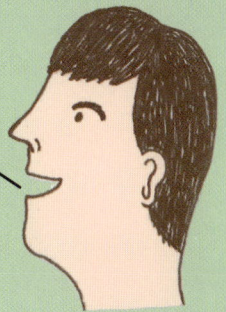

WHAT DO TWO COMPUTERS DO WHEN THEY LIKE EACH OTHER?

GO ON A DATA!

3. DELIVERY INSTRUCTIONS

Each data packet contains:

☑ **IP ADDRESSES** of the sender and recipient.

☑ Details about the packet's **CONTENTS**.

☑ **INSTRUCTIONS** to reassemble the data when the packets arrive.

DATA PACKETS

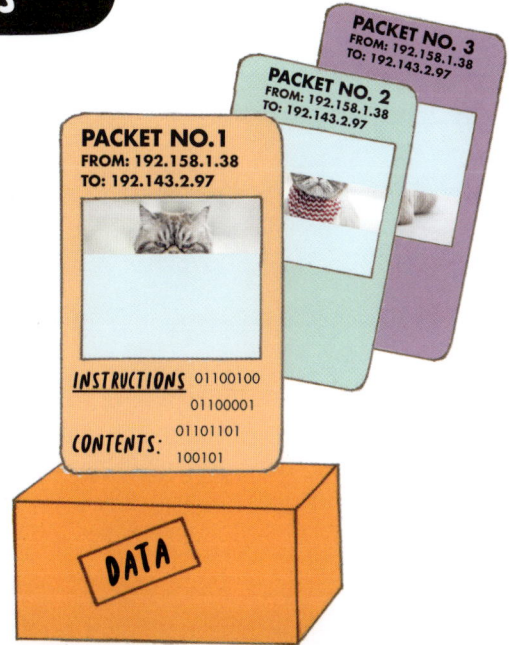

PACKET NO. 3
FROM: 192.158.1.38
TO: 192.143.2.97

PACKET NO. 2
FROM: 192.158.1.38
TO: 192.143.2.97

PACKET NO.1
FROM: 192.158.1.38
TO: 192.143.2.97

INSTRUCTIONS 01100100
01100001
CONTENTS: 01101101
100101

DATA

DATA PACKED AND READY TO GO!

Packets pass through **SERVERS**. These are like electronic post offices for data. They collect and then deliver data packets to their destination.

An email can travel halfway around the world in less than 0.2 seconds – that's faster than the blink of an eye!

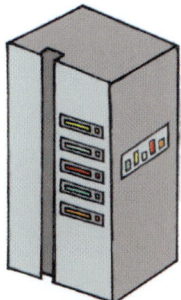

SERVER

IT'S YOU, TIDDLES!

Jess@coolmail.co.uk

Hi Sam,
Who does this cat remind you of? LOL

MEOW!

SPEEDY INTERNET

THANKS TO SHINY CABLES AND BOUNCING LIGHT BEAMS

BRAINIAC HACK: INTERNET CABLES

COPPER CABLE

FIBRE OPTIC CABLE

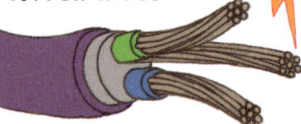

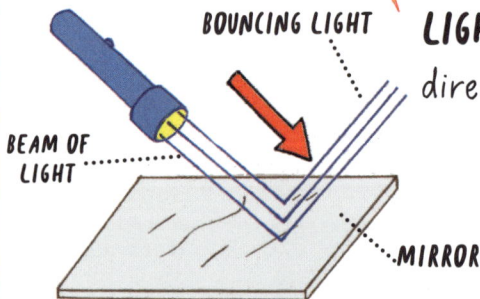

Cables connect many of us to the internet. **COPPER CABLES** transmit internet data as electric signals. **FIBRE OPTIC CABLES** are made from glass and use pulses of light to transmit data.

LIGHT travels very **FAST** in straight lines. It can change direction if it **BOUNCES** off shiny surfaces, like mirrors.

BOUNCING LIGHT

BEAM OF LIGHT

MIRROR

BOUNCING LIGHT

INSIDE FIBRE OPTIC CABLE

CASING STOPS LIGHT ESCAPING AND PROTECTS THE CABLE

The inside of each hair-thin fibre optic cable is like a mirror. Light bounces back and forth off the walls all the way along.

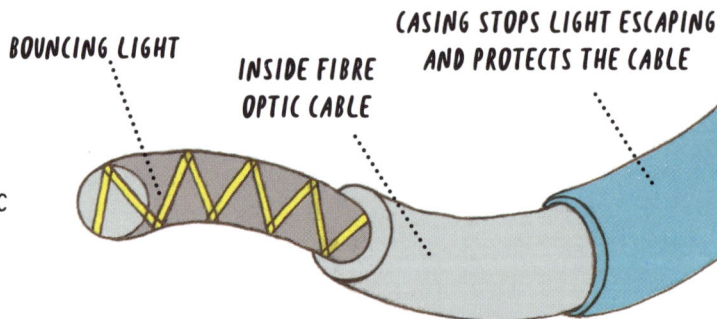

INSIDE FIBRE OPTIC CABLE

GUESS WHAT?
JAPAN HOLDS THE WORLD RECORD FOR THE FASTEST INTERNET SPEED – 402 TERABITS PER SECOND. THAT'S FAST ENOUGH TO DOWNLOAD 12,500 MOVIES IN LESS THAN THE BLINK OF AN EYE!

WHOA! IT'S FAST!

Fibre optic cables carry data quickly over long distances. This means a speedy internet connection.

<< FLIP BACK TO PAGE 10 TO FIND OUT ABOUT THE FIRST COMMUNICATION CABLES

TRAVELLING LIGHT

See how light travels by bouncing off a reflective surface.

YOU'LL NEED: an empty, clear plastic bottle, a bright torch, aluminium foil, sticky tape, a dark room with a sink

1. Wrap aluminium foil tightly around the plastic bottle, leaving the top and bottom of the bottle uncovered.

2. Fill the bottle with water. Switch off the light and switch on the torch.

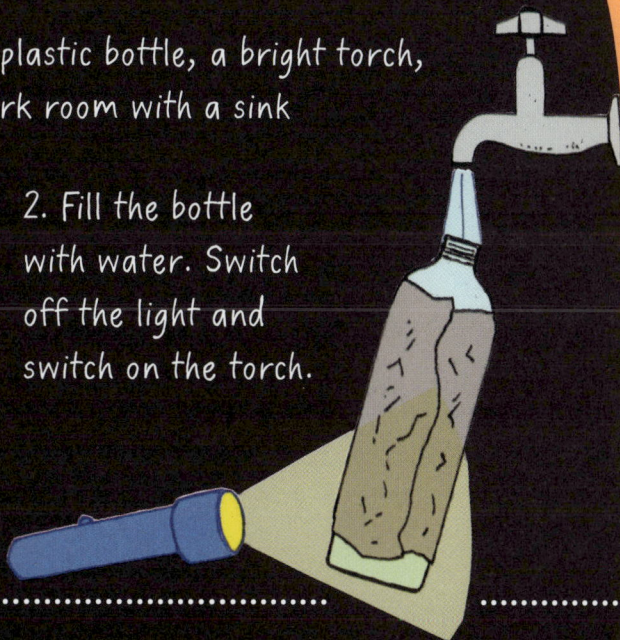

3. Press the torch against the bottom of the bottle.

4. Tilt the bottle so the water starts to pour out into the sink. Keep the torch pressed tight against the bottle. You should see the spout of water lighting up!

TOP TIP: IF YOU CAN'T SEE MUCH LIGHT IN THE WATER SPOUT, TRY A BRIGHTER TORCH.

EXPLANATION: The light from the torch is reflected as it bounces off the edge of the stream of water. The water carries the light, bending the light beam.

DATA DUMP

CYBER SPAGHETTI

NO INTERNET? BLAME BOATS, WILDLIFE OR THE WEATHER

Cables keep the world connected, but they are under attack!

ANCHORS AWAY!

Fishing nets and boat anchors dragging along the seabed cause costly cable breaks. Special ships rush to repair the damage as fast as possible.

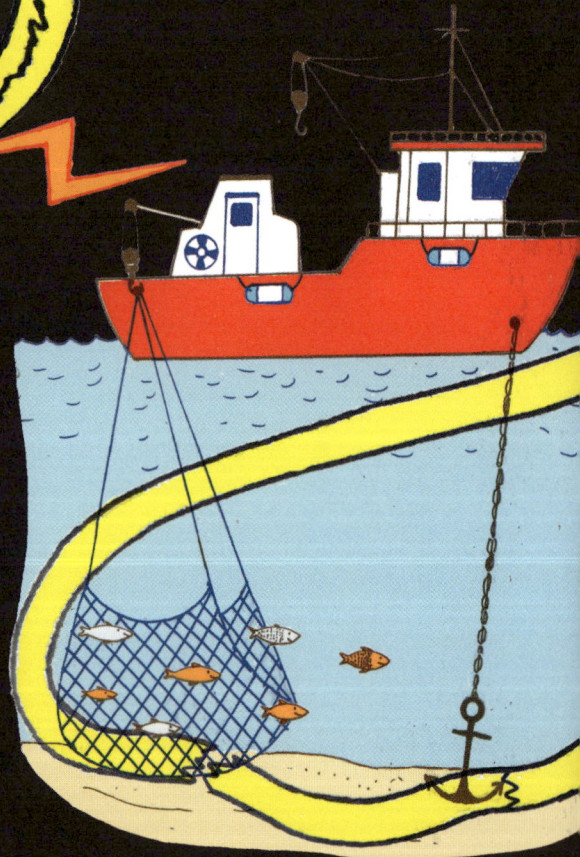

WILD WEATHER

Landslides and floods can uncover buried cables and lightning strikes can knock out the net. Even freezing temperatures and snow storms can snap cables.

THE WET NET

Hundreds of internet cables, many no thicker than a hosepipe, snake under the ocean for over 1,126,540km. That's long enough to circle the Earth 27 times!

MEGA BITES

Underwater cables are wrapped in a tough casing to protect them from sharks. Theses hungry hunters may mistake the electric charge coming from cables for fishy prey and try to take a bite.

NUTTY NIBBLERS

Cable-chewing creatures around the world cause millions of dollars of internet outages. They include rats in the UK, monkeys in India, beavers in Canada and gophers and raccoons in the USA. Squirrels are the worst offenders of all.

YUCK!

Some companies have tried adding hot spice and foul flavours to cable coverings to put off peckish pests.

BORING BUGS

Chirpy bugs called cicadas sometimes mistake overhead cables for tree branches. The females bore holes and lay their eggs inside the costly cables.

If the internet crashes, hop over to Google and pass the time offline playing their Dinosaur Game. Help T-Rex jump over cactuses and duck pterodactyls!

DIG IT

Underground cables carrying our data are everywhere. In 2012 a Georgian woman cut off internet access across the whole of Armenia after slicing through the main cable with her spade.

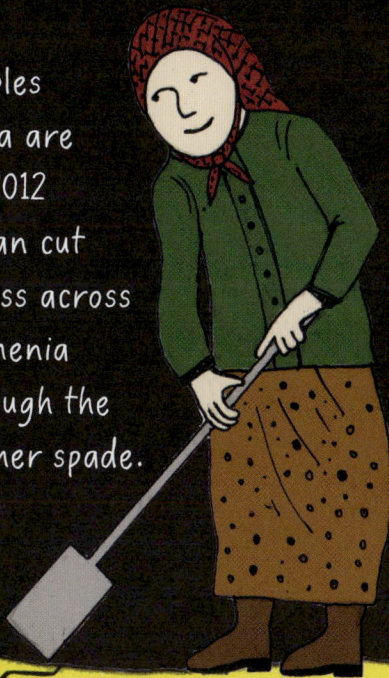

DATA UPS AND DOWNS

FAST OR SLOW, HIGH OR LOW, HOW DOES DATA FLOW?

You can watch or listen to content on the internet by **STREAMING** or **DOWNLOADING**.

DOWNLOADS are like a bath – you have to wait until the tub fills up before you can enjoy a soak.

When you download content, files are **COPIED** and **SAVED** onto your device. The entire file has to be copied before it can be opened.

STREAMING is like a shower – you jump straight in, but the water flows away.

To stream content, data is broken into **PACKETS** that are delivered one after another. Once watched or listened to, the data is **DELETED**.

I LIKE TO SOAK IT ALL IN

I LIKE TO GO WITH THE FLOW

✔ NO NEED FOR AN INTERNET CONNECTION ONCE IT IS DOWNLOADED
✔ YOU CAN PLAY THE FILE AGAIN AND AGAIN
✗ TAKES TIME TO DOWNLOAD
✗ TAKES UP MEMORY ON YOUR DEVICE

✔ YOU CAN START PLAYING IT STRAIGHT AWAY
✔ DOES NOT TAKE MUCH SPACE ON YOUR DEVICE
✔ YOU CAN WATCH LIVE EVENTS AS THEY HAPPEN
✗ ONLY WORKS WITH AN INTERNET CONNECTION

<< FLIP BACK TO PAGE 30 TO FIND OUT ABOUT DATA PACKETS

READY AND WAITING

When you stream content, a few seconds of the video or audio file is preloaded – this is known as **BUFFERING**. It means the content plays without stuttering and stalling if the internet is slow.

CURRENT POSITION **BUFFER (ALREADY LOADED)** **NOT YET LOADED**

In June, 1993, American garage rock band Severe Tire Damage became the first band to livestream on the internet. They were seen and heard live as far away as Australia!

HEAVY TRAFFIC

Does the internet slow down when all of your household are online at the same time? Things like online gaming and streaming videos uses a lot of data, so the **DELIVERY** system can get **JAMMED**.

HOW MUCH data can be transferred at a time is called **BANDWIDTH**. If data were cars, bandwidth would be the road...

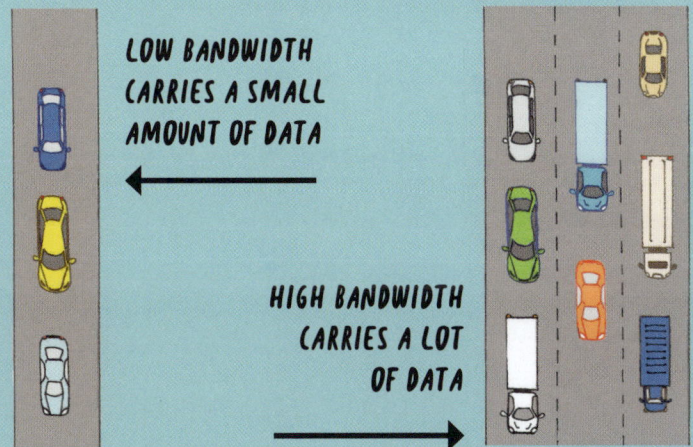

LOW BANDWIDTH CARRIES A SMALL AMOUNT OF DATA

HIGH BANDWIDTH CARRIES A LOT OF DATA

People pay more to have an internet connection with high **BANDWIDTH**.

TRY THIS

Check **HOW FAST** data can be transferred on your connection by doing an **INTERNET SPEED TEST**.

On a mobile phone, PC or tablet, do a search for 'internet speed test' to find a website – speedtest.net is a popular one.

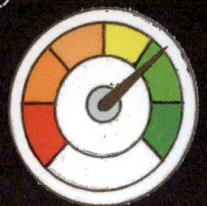

A WORLD WITHOUT WIRES

INVISIBLE WORDS, PICTURES AND SOUNDS ARE FLYING THROUGH THE AIR

RADIO WAVES

NEED-TO-KNOW FACTS

WI-FI connects nearby devices to the **INTERNET** without the need for cables or wires. It uses **RADIO WAVES.**

RADIO WAVES are harmless, invisible waves of energy that travel through the air. They are used for transmitting TV and radio programmes, too.

A **WIRELESS ROUTER** turns the **DATA** (sounds, pictures and words) from the internet into radio signals and sends them out into the airwaves.

Inside your devices a **WIRELESS ADAPTOR** picks up the radio signals and turns them back into data.

The router also sends data from your devices to the internet.

WHERE DID THE WI-FI ROUTER GO?

HE WENT DATA WAY!

MORE WIRELESS WONDERS

Radio waves are connecting us in all sorts of ways...

NFC (Near Field Communication) allows mobile phones and cards fitted with special microchips to transfer data with one tap. NFC is used for digital travel tickets, making payments and more.

Bluetooth was named after the Viking king Harold 'Bluetooth' Gormsson who united Denmark and Norway in 958 CE. The king got his nickname from his rotten, blue tooth!

BLUETOOTH connects electronic devices such as mobile phones, headphones and speakers over short distances. When two Bluetooth devices connect, it is called 'pairing'.

>> FLIP FORWARD TO PAGE 58 TO SEE WHO INVENTED WIRELESS TECHNOLOGY

INTERNET IN YOUR POCKET

WHEREVER WE GO, MINI COMPUTERS KEEP US CONNECTED

Hello? Hello?! In 1973, American engineer Martin Cooper made the first mobile phone call. The phone was the size of a brick, the battery only lasted for 30 minutes and it took 10 hours to recharge!

Today we have **SMARTPHONES** that are like mini computers. They run programs, called **APPS**, which allow us do an endless list of things, from fitness routines to surfing the net.

THIS IS APP-STOUNDING!

TRY THIS

MAKING WAVES

Mobile phones communicate by sending and receiving **RADIO WAVES**.

While switched on, mobile phones send out **INVISIBLE** radio waves. The waves travel in all directions, like ripples in water.

To see how radio waves travel, fill a washing up bowl with water. Drop a pebble into the centre of the bowl and watch the ripples spread out.

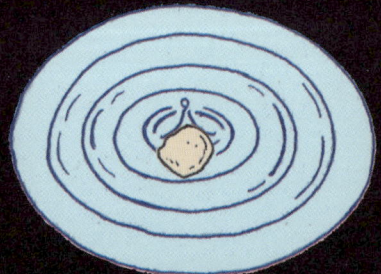

MOBILE INTERNET

A **SMARTPHONE** can connect to the internet wherever there is a good **SIGNAL**.

1. To connect to the internet a mobile phone needs to communicate with a mast, called a base station.

2. Base stations are dotted around the country. A local base station picks up the phone's radio signals.

3. The base station connects to the internet by underground cables.

I'LL JUST CHECK THE WEATHER APP

1
4
2
3

BASE STATION MAST

BASE STATION

UNDERGROUND CABLE

4. Data is sent back to the base station, which transmits it as radio signals to the phone.

SEARCH FOR A SIGNAL

If you are on the move, your phone connects to the next base station.

LET ME CHECK THE MAP

WHAT A VIEW!

Or you might be too far from a base station to pick up a signal.

I CAN'T FIND A SIGNAL

Buildings, hills and even trees can block radio waves.

SMART STUFF

CLEVER TECH MAKES LIFE SIMPLE

SMART DEVICES are packed with clever technology. They might use AI (Artificial Intelligence) to learn your routine, or be programmed to perform tasks for themselves.

All smart devices have a **WIRELESS INTERNET CONNECTION** so they can communicate and be controlled remotely by a smartphone.

LOOK SMART

Work out what these smart devices are, then find them in the house.

1 TELL IT WHAT YOU NEED TO KNOW OR WANT TO HEAR. IT BROWSES THE NET TO BRING YOU FACTS AND TRACKS.

2 HELP OUT IN THE GARDEN WITHOUT LIFTING A FINGER – OR EVEN STEPPING OUTSIDE!

3 SYNC THIS DEVICE TO YOUR MUSIC FOR AN INSTANT DISCO. PLUS, PHONE APP CONTROLS MEAN NO MORE FUMBLING IN THE DARK FOR SWITCHES.

4 WATCH A COOKERY SHOW, OPEN THE DOOR AND GRAB THE INGREDIENTS.

7 CAN'T FIND THE REMOTE? CHANGE CHANNELS WITH YOUR PHONE, STREAM VIDEOS AND MUSIC OR SURF THE NET.

8 FEED TIDDLES ON TIME WITHOUT HAVING TO STOP WHAT YOU ARE DOING.

9 OOPS! A TEXT ALERT FROM THIS DEVICE COULD MEAN THERE'S A FIRE – OR SOMEONE BURNT THE TOAST.

HOPE I HAVE ENOUGH PAPER

AS WELL AS SMART DEVICES, THERE ARE 3 OTHER WIRELESS CONNECTIONS TO SPOT.

Phew! My watch says I have run 3 miles and done 35,000 steps. Spider steps count 8 times!

5 FORGOT YOUR KEY? USE YOUR FINGERPRINT.

6 THIS CLEANS UP WHILE YOU PUT YOUR FEET UP.

OUT OF THIS WORLD

SATELLITES CIRCLING IN SPACE CONNECT PEOPLE ON EARTH... AND BEYOND

NEED-TO-KNOW FACTS

Underground cables cannot reach remote locations, so many people are connected to the internet by **SATELLITE**.

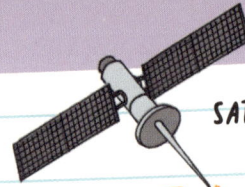

SATELLITE

3 THE SIGNAL IS BEAMED BACK TO EARTH

2 THE SIGNAL IS BEAMED TO A SATELLITE

1 CABLES DELIVER THE INTERNET TO AN ANTENNA CALLED A GROUND STATION

4

THE SIGNAL IS CAPTURED BY AN ANTENNA (DISH) ATTACHED TO THE BUILDING

MICROWAVES are used to send signals to and from satellites because **EARTH'S ATMOSPHERE** blocks weaker radio waves.

SATELLITE

EARTH'S ATMOSPHERE

RADIO WAVES

MICROWAVES

TRANSMITTER

SATELLITE INTERNET

<< FLIP BACK TO PAGE 38 TO FIND OUT MORE ABOUT RADIO WAVES

NASA IS LAUNCHING A SATELLITE TO SAY SORRY TO THE ALIENS.

THEY ARE CALLING IT THE APOLLO G.

WE HAVE LIFT OFF!

Now the net is heading into the cosmos...

FAR OUT!

Internet signals travel at the speed of light, but the round-trip for communications from Earth to Mars can take between 7 to 40 minutes, depending on the location of Mars relative to Earth (the planets are always moving!).

SPACE WIDE WEB

The best science and technology brains are preparing for manned missions to Mars by building an interplanetary internet. A network of satellites will connect Earth to space probes and space travellers.

The internet has already been beamed to the Moon with powerful lasers. Wi-fi will make it easy to communicate with and control lunar rovers from Earth. Also, astronauts will be able to watch YouTube!

NO SPACE!

Over 6,000 satellites have already been launched by Elon Musk's SpaceX company to bring internet to remote parts of the planet. They join thousands of other communication satellites whizzing around overhead.

WACKY WI-FI!

DATA DUMP

WILD RIDES, WI-FI IN THE SKY AND HOTSPOTS WITH HOOVES

Discover some of the clever and crazy ideas that have helped to get people online.

WI-FI HOTSPOTS make it possible to connect to the internet when you are on the go. There are more than **50 MILLION** hotspots across the world!

WI-FI SIGNS TO LOOK OUT FOR

SKY-FI

In the 2010s, Google's Project Loon sent special solar-powered balloons soaring 20 kilometres into the sky. They successfully beamed internet down to the most remote areas on the planet.

HUBS WITH HUMPS

In some of the world's deserts, herds of camels are being turned into mobile internet hubs. Camels wander across the dusty dunes carrying routers, allowing nomadic people to get online.

WHEELY HIGH

It's double the fun on a Ferris wheel at Yomiuriland amusement park in Tokyo, Japan. Wi-fi-enabled pods mean people can work, browse or game while doing leisurely loops 60 metres up in the air.

FLY-FI

A safari park in Chessington, England, used macaws to get people connected. The tropical birds were trained to clutch routers in their claws and beaks as they swooped over the park.

SOCIAL DONKEYS

A theme park in Israel takes visitors on a journey back to biblical times. It kitted donkeys out with wi-fi routers so tourists could snap and share their historic ride straight from the saddle.

GUESS WHAT?

A PERSONAL HOTSPOT IS <u>NOT</u> YOUR SWEATY ARMPITS! IT ALLOWS YOU TO SHARE A MOBILE INTERNET CONNECTION FROM A SMARTPHONE TO OTHER DEVICES.

CRACKABLE OR UNHACKABLE

KEEP YOUR INFO LOCKED AWAY WITH PUZZLING PASSWORDS

BRAINIAC HACK: PASSWORDS

Online accounts use **PASSWORDS** to keep your personal information safe.

MY DOG'S NAME WILL BE EASY TO REMEMBER

HACKERS can crack simple passwords in seconds using automated tools.

They use your information to **SCAM** you for money or **SPAM** you with adverts.

LET'S TRY PET NAMES... LIKE 'SPOT'. BINGO!

STRONG PASSWORDS

spot

sPotiSmYd09

sp*tiSmYd09U·U

The best passwords have **NUMBERS, SYMBOLS** and upper and lower case **LETTERS**. The longer and more complicated they are, the trickier they are to hack!

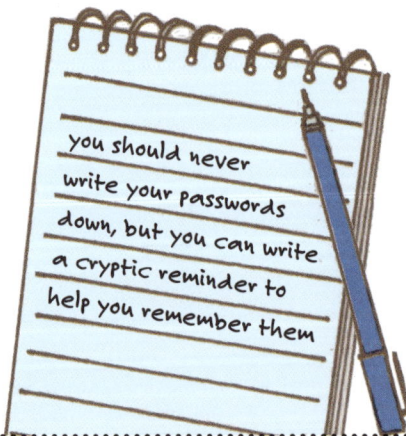

you should never write your passwords down, but you can write a cryptic reminder to help you remember them

REMEMBER ME?

Use the passwords function to securely store passwords for you. Only use this on a personal computer or device.

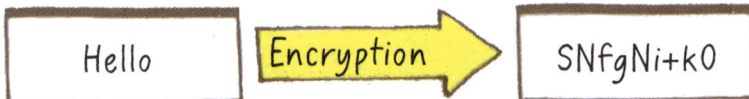

Hello → Encryption → SNfgNi+k0

They use **ENCRYPTION**. This is a type of **SECRET CODE** that scrambles text and gives your tricky password extra protection from criminals.

CREATE A PASSWORD

Create an unhackable password using these steps...

1. Pick a name, animal and object that you can remember.

CHLOE

CAT

CAPE

2. Use the numbered alphabet below to create your password.

A	B	C	D	E	F	G
1	2	3	4	5	6	7

H	I	J	K	L	M	N
8	9	10	11	12	13	14

O	P	Q	R	S	T	U
15	16	17	18	19	20	21

V	W	X	Y	Z
22	22	24	25	26

3. Replace every letter in the animal word with a number.

3120

4. Write every other letter of the name as a number.

c8l15e

5. Replace every vowel in the object with a number.

c1p5

6. Put the words next to each other, with a symbol of your choice between each word.

3120@c8l15e%c1p5$

7. Write out the whole password back-to-front.

$5p1c%e51l8c@0213

Congratulations! You just encrypted your password! Now challenge a volunteer to unscramble the words. When they give up, tell them how to do it and see how long it takes!

49

ONLINE SURVIVAL GUIDE

THE INTERNET IS A JUNGLE OF INFORMATION

Don't get in a tangle with fake facts, or fall into the trap of oversharing. Follow these tips...

WHAT! SOME NEWS STORIES ARE FAKE? I DON'T BELIEVE IT

STOP AND T.H.I.N.K

Does what you're reading, or what you're posting pass the **THINK TEST**?

T = IS IT TRUE?   If in doubt, check five trustworthy sources (online or offline).

H = IS IT HELPFUL?   Does it have a purpose? Can people learn from it or be entertained by it?

I = IS IT INSPIRING?   Does it say something new or add to a chat in an interesting way?

N = IS IT NECESSARY?   Is something being shared that should really be kept private?

K = IS IT KIND?   Could it be hurtful or upsetting to anyone?

DIGITAL FOOTPRINTS

Your online activity leaves a trail...

It is difficult to erase information once it has been put on the internet. Even if you **TAKE DOWN** a post or **DELETE** your account, your text, photo or video might be stored on a web server as data, or saved on somebody's device.

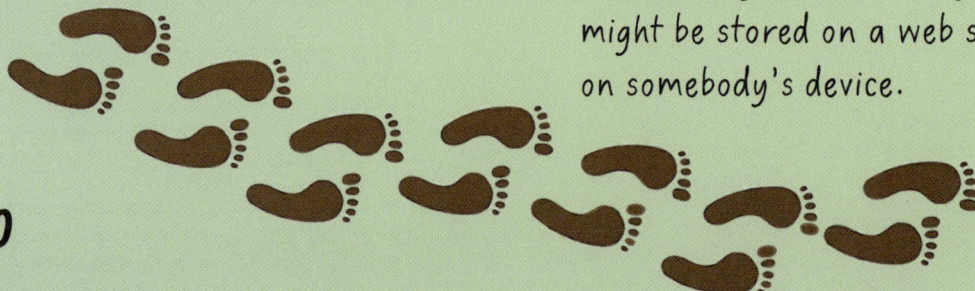

JAW-DROPPING!

NILE CROCODILES GET THEIR TEETH PICKED BY PLUCKY LITTLE PLOVER BIRDS!

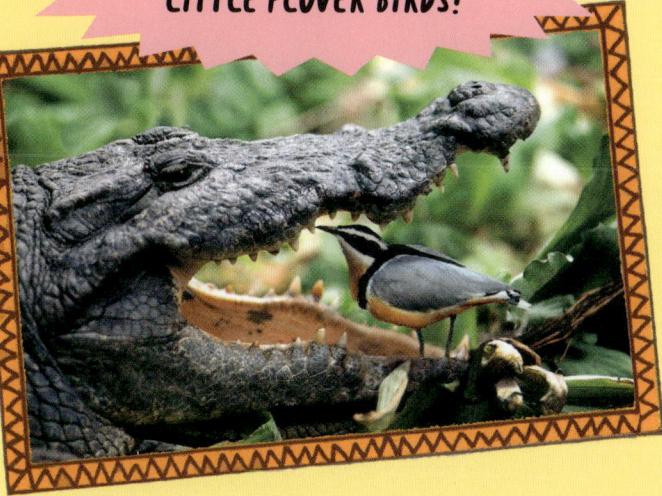

'The bite-sized birds feast on a free meaty meal and the crocs get a shiny set of deadly gnashers!'

CHECK THE FACTS

Type 'plover bird and crocodile' into a search engine and lots of results pop up, but **IS THIS STORY TRUE?**

WHERE? Are the sources trustworthy? (E.g. encyclopedias and museum sites).

WHO? Is the author an expert?

HOW? Is it written to grab attention?

FAMOUS FAKE

Beware of bears … and other digitally altered images.

FAKE

REAL

A group of wildlife photographers took a photo that shows them running for their lives, then added a grizzly bear using Photoshop. They posted it on Facebook to spook their friends, but it was so **DRAMATIC** that it went viral!

Thanks to clever photo editing tools and the way information spreads online, many people were fooled by these fake images. The plover bird story was shared on blogs and it even ended up in books!

AI DETECTIVE

HOW TO SPOT A BOT IN THE WILD

Now that artificial intelligence is connected to the internet, you need to know the difference between what's human and what's bot.

NEED-TO-KNOW FACTS

The term **ARTIFICIAL INTELLIGENCE** was first used in 1956 to describe machines that could solve problems like a human. AI was used to **PROGRAM MACHINES** to do automatic jobs in factories.

Computers were then taught **HOW TO THINK**. AI learned how to play chess against a human and how to drive a car on a busy road.

In the 2010s, computer scientists taught machines how to process large amounts of data. **GPUs (GRAPHICS PROCESSING UNITS)** became more effective at passing on information quickly. This was fantastic news for 3D video games.

Today, **CHAT BOTS** such as ChatGPT can **LEARN FOR THEMSELVES** - all they need is access to all the free information on the internet.

Computers have the brain power to **THINK** but they lack the emotions to **FEEL**. Although they can read emotions on a person's face, computers do not have the ability to feel **EMPATHY**, which is to imagine what someone else might be feeling.

BOT, OR NOT?

Chatbots are good at mimicking human behaviour, but they can make some telling mistakes. Here are some ways to spot whether content may be AI-generated:

HUMAN...

LANGUAGE

Tries to use words that others will understand:
'The sky is blue.'

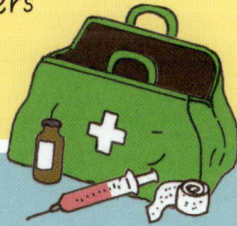

QUESTION & ANSWER

Can answer a question that has many possible answers:
'Will there be another pandemic?'
'It depends...'

INFORMATION

Often presents information as a story:
'On a rainy night in 1491, one of England's most powerful rulers was born...'

PICTURES

Makes a picture that is entirely original using the imagination.

CHATBOT...

LANGUAGE

May use flowery or old-fashioned words that are hard to understand:
'The sky is a rich palette of cobalt and azure.'

QUESTION & ANSWER

May struggle to answer a question that has many possible answers:
'Will there be another pandemic?'
'I cannot find that information.'

INFORMATION

Often presents information as a summary followed by bullet points:
'King Henry VIII reigned between 1509-1547.
> Henry VIII was born in England in 1491.
> Henry VIII was from the House of Tudor.'

PICTURES

Makes a picture by combining existing images, often in unusual or unbelievable ways.

JUST THE JOB

THE INTERNET NEEDS DIFFERENT PEOPLE DOING DIFFERENT JOBS

Building, designing or fixing - there's work on the internet whatever your skills!

ARE YOU A CREATIVE PROBLEM-SOLVER?

You could be a **WEB DESIGNER**.
Web designers make websites easy and fun to use. They study how people use the internet, and combine text, images and videos to make it better and faster.

DO YOU LOVE COMPUTERS AND CODING?

You could be a **PROGRAMMER**.
Programmers build websites from scratch using programs like HTML and Python. They test and fix bugs to improve the way websites work.

DO YOU LOVE MAKING AND MENDING THINGS?

You could be a **BROADBAND ENGINEER**.
Engineers get out and about in the physical world to keep people online. They fix faults and install fibre optic cables to connect homes and offices to the internet.

The internet is like a cake that is made up of layers of technology. If the technology on one layer stops working, the whole internet stops working. Working on the internet involves collaboration...

LET'S EAT INTERNET CAKE!

Each internet job provides a service to the layer above it and below it.

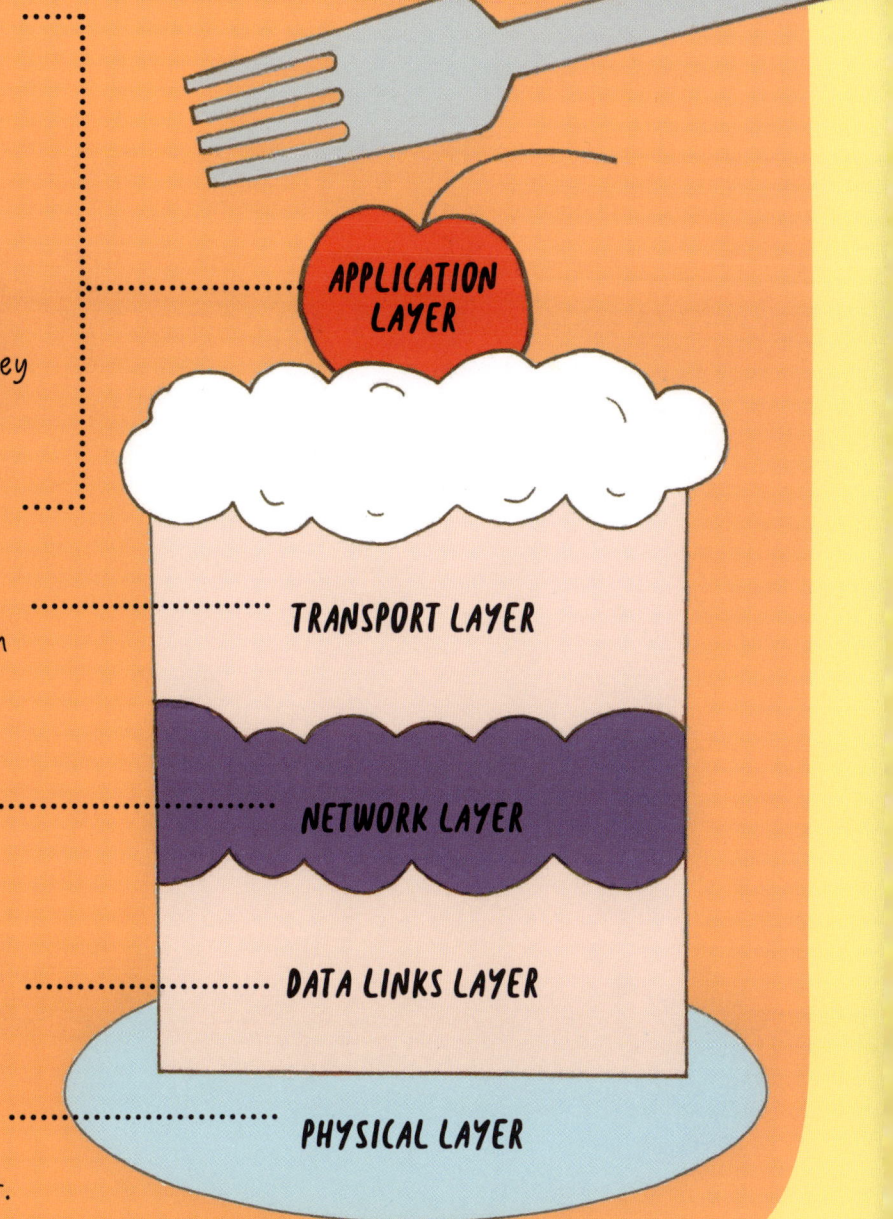

WEB PROGRAMMERS create web pages and apps that format data in a way that internet users can understand.

SOFTWARE ENGINEERS create code for websides and apps, and can also create code to encrypt and de-encrypt data so that devices can run more efficiently. They also maintain sessions of communication so that two devices can stay connected on the internet.

PROTOCOL ENGINEERS can create new technologies to send data in packets from one part of the internet to another.

COMMUNICATION ENGINEERS create new ways to transfer data between devices on different networks and...

... improve the transfer of data between devices on the same network.

NETWORK ENGINEERS can create new technologies to optimise data transfer from systems and devices to the internet.

APPLICATION LAYER

TRANSPORT LAYER

NETWORK LAYER

DATA LINKS LAYER

PHYSICAL LAYER

EXCITING TIMES!

DATA DUMP

IN JUST A FEW DECADES, THE INTERNET HAS CHANGED OUR LIVES

Time flies when you're Googling, surfing, texting and blogging!

In 1995, less than one percent of the world's population had an internet connection. Today there are 5.44 billion internet users – that's 67 percent of the people on Earth. The world is changing so fast, that by the time you read these facts, they will ALL BE OUT OF DATE!

69,400 Taylor Swift songs are streamed.

41,600,000 WhatsApp messages are sent.

241 million emails are sent.

1,110 Amazon packages are sent for delivery.

6.94 million emojis are sent.

More than 500 hours of video is uploaded to YouTube.

16 million texts are sent.

JUST A MINUTE!

A lot happens in **60 SECONDS** on the internet **EVERY MINUTE.**

INTERNET TIMELINE

1991
WORLD WIDE WEB MADE PUBLIC FOR FREE

FREE!

1998
FIRST INTERNET SEARCH LAUNCHES

2002
FIRST CLOUD COMPUTING LAUNCHES

2005
FIRST ONLINE VIDEO PLATFORM LAUNCHES

UNDER CONSTRUCTION

The internet will never stop growing and evolving. More big changes lie ahead!

Work is underway to take the internet to Mars and the rest of the **SOLAR SYSTEM**.

6 HOURS AND 35 MINUTES

The average amount of time that people spend online each day – that's like a whole school day!

200,000 YEARS

How long modern humans have existed on Earth. The internet has only been around for about 40 years.

Scientists are developing an **UNDERWATER INTERNET** that will provide wi-fi under the waves.

SWIPE!

SWIPE!

OVER TO YOU!

All netizens (people who use the internet) have a responsibility to treat the internet and other users with respect. Let's keep the net a caring, happy place to share our news and views.

BETWEEN 8 AND 44 MINUTES

The time it takes to send a message from Earth to Mars varies depending on where Mars is in its orbit.

The future of the internet is in your hands, it will be whatever you make it.

2007
FIRST MOVIE
STREAMS ONLINE

2016
ONLINE TEXT
EDITING LAUNCHES

2019
5G CONNECTIVITY
LAUNCHES

2022
AI IS CONNECTED
TO THE INTERNET

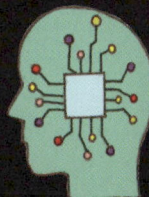

WHAT'S NEXT?

INTERNET HALL OF FAME

MEET THE BRAINIACS WHO HELPED BUILD THE INTERNET

In 1837, **CHARLES BABBAGE** drew up plans for a clockwork calculating machine called the Analytical Engine.

MY DESIGNS WERE USED TO BUILD THE FIRST COMPUTER.

I WAS THE FIRST COMPUTER PROGRAMMER.

WE WERE THE BRAINS BEHIND WIRELESS TECHNOLOGY.

In 1842, mathematician **ADA LOVELACE** created a way to instruct the Analytical Engine to solve more complicated problems – it was the first computer program!

As well as being inventors, Hedy Lamarr was a Hollywood actress and George Antheil was a composer. Multi-talented, like me!

In 1942, inventors **HEDY LAMARR** and **GEORGE ANTHEIL** created a system that used radio waves to send messages. Their ideas were the basis for wi-fi and bluetooth.

MY WORK MADE IT EASIER FOR PEOPLE TO LEARN PROGRAMMING.

In the 1950s, computer scientist **GRACE HOPPER** had the idea of creating a computer language that used words instead of complicated symbols. The result was COBOL, one of the most widely used computer codes ever!

Computer scientist and network engineer **RADIA PERLMAN** made it possible for the internet to move more data, more quickly.

IF I AM SUCCESSFUL, THE STUFF I DESIGN NOBODY WILL EVER NOTICE. THINGS WILL JUST WORK.

Without the rules, or protocols, invented by **VINT CERF** and **BOB KAHN** we would not be able to send data using the internet.

THE WEB DOES NOT JUST CONNECT MACHINES, IT CONNECTS PEOPLE.

TIM BERNERS-LEE sat down and wrote the code for the world wide web over 30 years ago. He could never have dreamed that his invention for sharing information would end up changing the world!

PROF. DR LARISSA SUZUKI has worked for Google and NASA. Since 2020 she has been helping to create the interplanetary internet, a project that will take the internet into space.

At the moment, she is working on technology that will allow astronauts to operate spacecraft using their voices!

I'M A COMPUTER SCIENTIST, ENGINEER, INVENTOR... AND THE AUTHOR OF THIS BOOK!

GLOSSARY

APPS
Programs connected to the internet, that perform a specific task, and are usually accessed on a mobile device.

ARTIFICIAL INTELLIGENCE (AI)
Computer programming that can learn and adapt independently, allowing machines to do more complex jobs.

ARTIFICIAL SATELLITE
An object or machine built by humans and sent into space to travel around the Earth.

BANDWIDTH
The maximum amount of data that can be sent across a network at a time.

BINARY
A number system that uses just the digits 0 and 1 to encode information so that computers can then process it.

BLOG
Written web-content, usually related to a particular subject or interest, usually created by one or a small team of people.

CHATBOT
A computer program that uses AI to simulate human conversations.

CODE
A language used by programmers to give instructions to computers.

COMPUTER PROGRAM
A list of instructions a computer follows in order to process information and perform tasks.

CONTENT
Words, images, videos and audio created and uploaded to the internet, to be accessed by other internet users.

DATA
Information stored on and sent between electronic devices, such as computers, tablets and smartphones.

DIGITAL
Relating to information that has been turned into 0s and 1s (binary).

ENCRYPTION

The process of turning data into a complicated code to keep it private.

INTERNET

A world-wide network that any computer can connect to.

GPS (GLOBAL POSITIONING SYSTEM)

A network of satellites in space that send out signals, which can be used with digital maps to determine where you are.

HYPERLINK

A link from one web page to another, activated by clicking on a specific word or image.

LIVESTREAM

ILive video or audio content broadcast over the internet.

NETWORK

Two or more computers that are able to communicate with each other electronically.

PROTOCOLS

Rules used in computer programming.

ROUTER

A device that receives and transmits internet data over short distances, such as within a house.

SERVER

A powerful computer that provides information to and stores information from other computers connected to its network.

URL

A website's address, which allows a browser to find and display the website to the user.

WEB BROWSER

A computer application used to access websites.

WEB FEED

The series of content that is shown to you on a website or app.

WORLD WIDE WEB

A series of online websites and documents, which can be linked together by hyperlinks and can be accessed by anyone connected to the internet.

WE WANT ANSWERS!

16 – INTERNET TREASURE HUNT

1. https://science.nasa.gov/mission/hubble/multimedia/
   what-did-hubble-see-on-your-birthday
2. https://girlswhocode.com/programs/code-at-home
3. Draw with Rob 21, Football panda: https://www.youtube.com/
   watch?v=CIKY8IzM1Is

27 – CRACK THE CODE

Answer: A keyboard

42 – LOOK SMART

1. SMART voice assistant
2. SMART lawn mower
3. SMART bulb
4. SMART fridge
5. SMART door lock
6. SMART vacuum
7. SMART TV
8. SMART pet feeder
9. SMART smoke alarm

DID YOU ALSO SPOT THE FOLLOWING?

10. Wi-fi router
11. Tablet
12. Bluetooth speaker

FIND OUT MORE...

If you'd like to find out more about the internet and what it's like
to work with the internet, visit these sites:

https://www.scienceandmediamuseum.org.uk/objects-and-stories/short-history-internet
https://www.internethalloffame.org
https://www.computerhistory.org

INDEX

PROF. DR LARISSA SUZUKI

is a computer scientist, engineer, author and inventor.
She holds a PhD in computer science from UCL, an MPhil
in electrical engineering and a bachelor's degree in computer
science. She currently works as a visiting scientist at
NASA JPL, as an honorary associate professor at UCL
and a technical director in the Office of the CTO at Google.
She is an advocate for increasing diversity in engineering,
especially for people with disabilities and neurodiversity.

HARRIET RUSSELL

is an illustrator of books for children, including the
bestselling *This Book Thinks You're a Scientist*, published
by Thames & Hudson. *The Brainiac's Book of the Internet*
is her 20th illustrated children's book.

First published in the United Kingdom in 2025 by Thames & Hudson Ltd,
181A High Holborn, London WC1V 7QX

The Brainiac's Book of the Internet © 2025 Thames & Hudson Ltd

Text © 2025 Prof. Dr Larissa Suzuki
Illustrations © 2025 Harriet Russell

Edited by Cath Ard

British Library Cataloguing-in-Publication Data
A catalogue record for this book is available from the British Library

ISBN 978-0-500-65309-8

Impression 01

Printed and bound in China by RR Donnelley

FSC
www.fsc.org
MIX
Paper | Supporting
responsible forestry
FSC® C144853

Be the first to know about our new releases,
exclusive content and author events by visiting
thamesandhudson.com
thamesandhudsonusa.com
thamesandhudson.com.au

Photography credits
a = above; b = below; c = centre; l = left; r = right

page 8: jalala/Getty Images
page 12br: Mary Evans/Everett Collection
page 12ar: Science History Images/Alamy
page 12bl: David J. Green - electrical/Alamy
page 12al: CYLU/Shutterstock
page 13 (clockwise from top left): Nowwy Jirawat/Shutterstock;
ranplett/Getty Images; Audio und werbung/Shutterstock;
Lastroll/Shutterstock; NYC Russ/Shutterstock; McLittle Stock/
Shutterstock; Tatyana Azarova/Alamy
page 30al, ar, bl: Lisa Charbonneau/Shutterstock
page 30cl: Nils Jacobi/Shutterstock
page 31a, b: Lisa Charbonneau/Shutterstock
page 51l: Juniors Bildarchiv GmbH/Alamy
page 51ar: Courtesy Teo Vladimirov⬜
page 51br: FreeImages.com/Photo soikha
page 58al: Pictorial Press Ltd/Alamy
page 58ar: incamerastock/Alamy
page 58cl: ScreenProd/Photononstop/Alamy
page 58c: Bettmann/Getty Images
page 58bl: Science History Images / Alamy
page 59 (clockwise from top left): Mpi43/Media Punch/Alamy Live News;
© Xu Jinquan/Xinhua/Alamy; Scientist-100 at English Wikipedia;
Oliver Berg/dpa/Alamy; Lara Suzuki

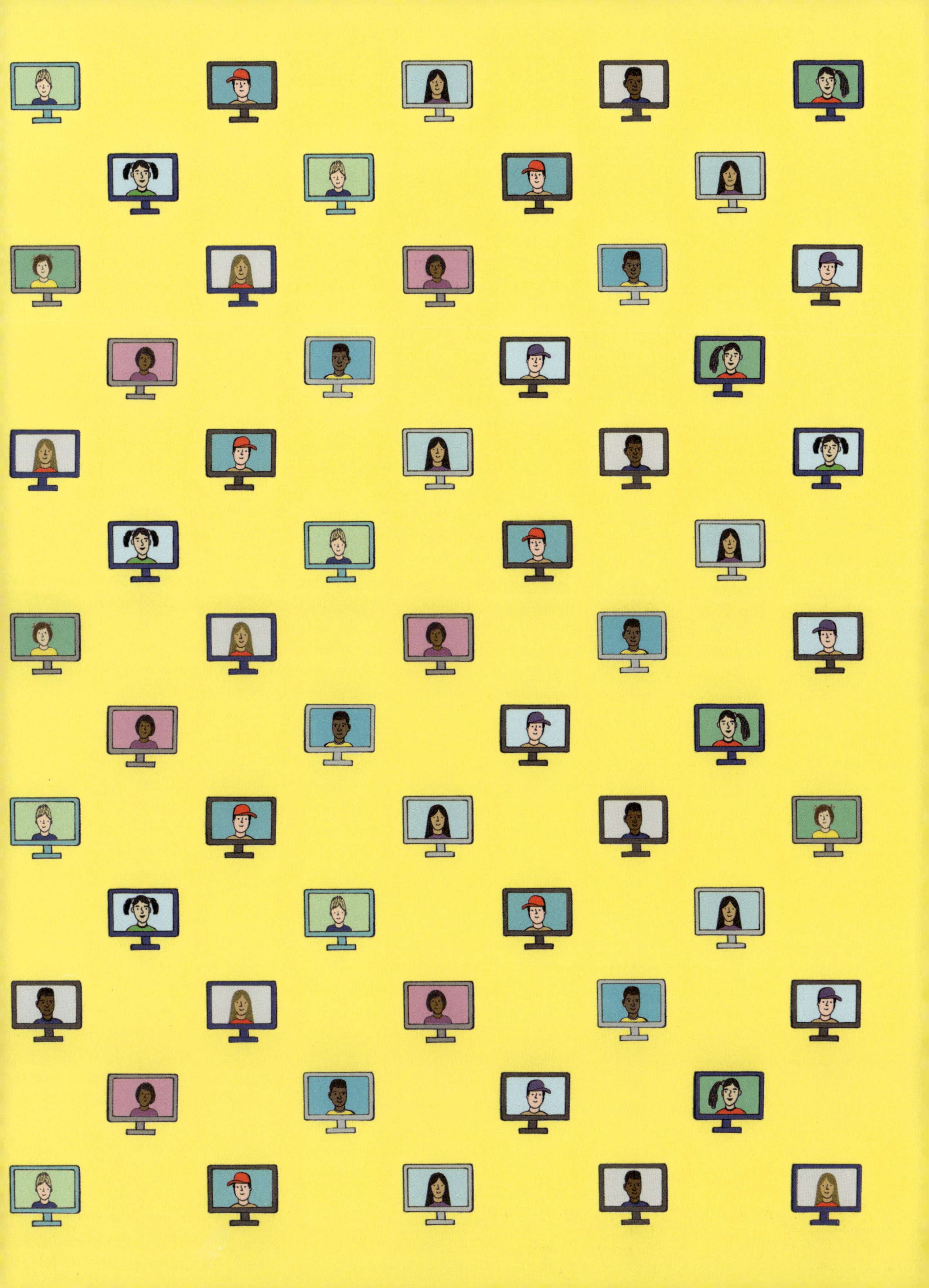

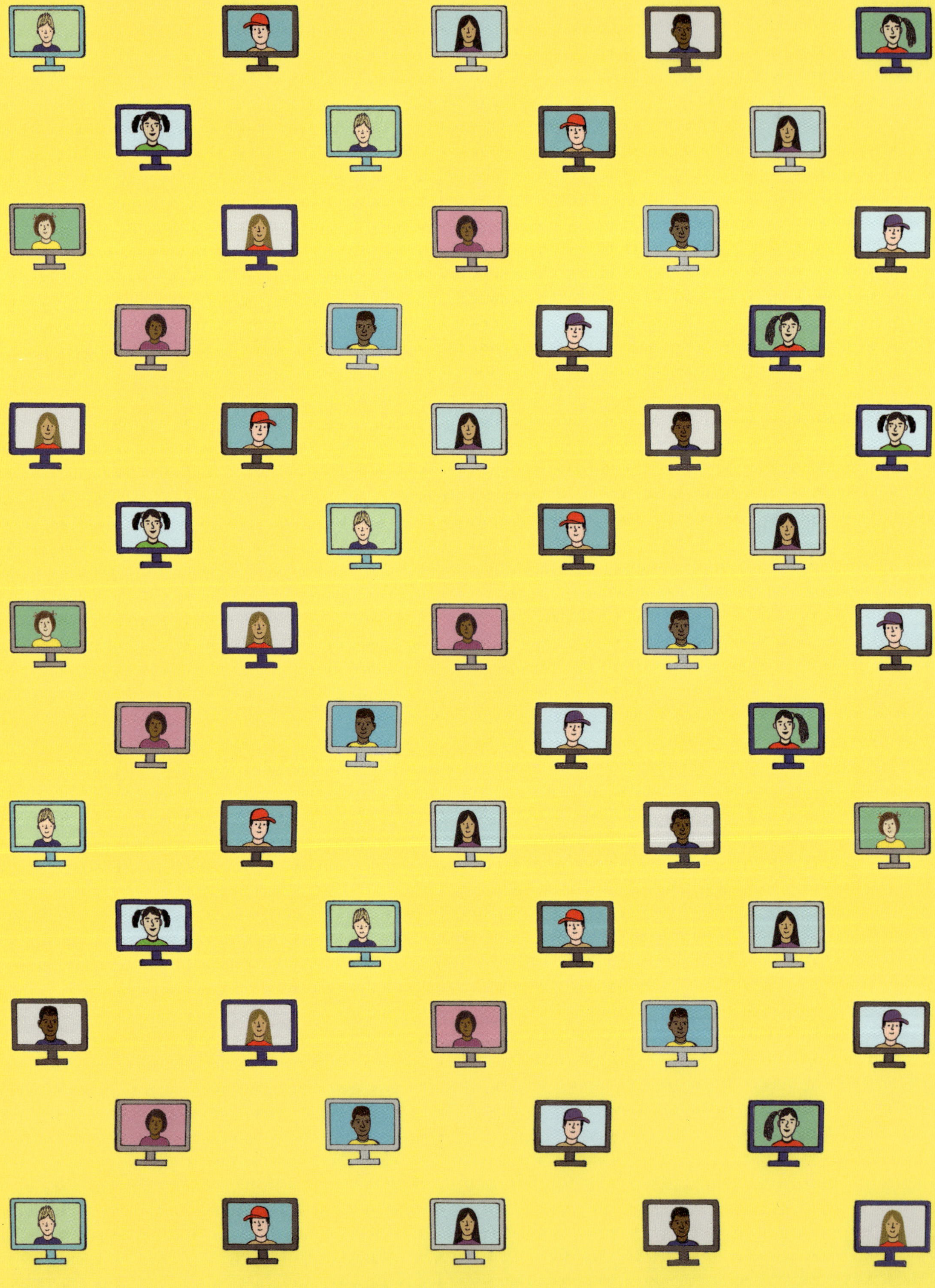